10 MINUTE SATs TESTS
READING

T0326067

AGES 7-8
YEAR 3

KS2

Scholastic Education, an imprint of Scholastic Ltd

Book End, Range Road, Witney, Oxfordshire, OX29 0YD

Registered office: Westfield Road, Southam, Warwickshire CV47 0RA

www.scholastic.co.uk

© 2018, Scholastic Ltd

3 4 5 6 7 8 9   8 9 0 1 2 3 4 5 6 7

British Library Cataloguing-in-Publication Data

A catalogue record for this book is available from the British Library.

ISBN 978-1407-17520-1

Printed and bound in India by Replika Press Pvt. Ltd.

Author
Wendy Jolliffe

Editorial
Rachel Morgan, Audrey Stokes, Kate Pedlar, Louise Titley

Series Design
Scholastic Design Team: Nicolle Thomas and Neil Salt

Design
Scholastic Design Team: Neil Salt

Cover Design
Dipa Mistry

Cover Illustration
Claudia Souza @ The Bright Agency

Illustrations
Gareth Llewhellin @ The Bright Agency; page 24 Sami Sweeten

Photographs
page 20: children, FatCamera/iStock; water bottle, F-91/iStock; page 21:
fruit and vegetables, boschettophotography/iStock; egg, EricFerguson/
iStock; page 27 and page 28: cliff, jremes84/iStock; page 39: polar bear,
Mario_Hoppmann/iStock; page 43: volcano, Beboy_ltd/iStock

Contents

How to use this book

This book contains ten different Reading tests for Year 3, each containing SATs-style questions. As a whole, the complete set of tests provides broad coverage of the test framework for this age group. Each test comprises a text followed by comprehension questions. The texts cover a wide range of subject matter across the three key areas: fiction, non-fiction and poetry.

Some questions require a selected response, where children choose the correct answer from several options. Other questions require a constructed response, where children write a short or extended answer of their own. Guidance on the different question types and the skills needed to deal with them is covered on pages 53 to 61.

A mark scheme and a progress chart are also included towards the end of this book.

Completing the tests

- It is intended that children will take approximately ten minutes to complete each test.

- After your child has completed a test, mark it and together identify and practise any areas where your child is less confident. Ask them to complete the next test at a later date, when you feel they have had enough time to practise and improve.

Ben and Buster

Ben's best friend was Buster the dog. He was supposed to be a cockapoo, which is a mix of a poodle and a cocker spaniel. Buster's coat was too curly and his ears weren't right, but Ben loved him. Buster was funny. He would run around in circles chasing his tail. He would bark at the trees when it was windy. He loved to play ball with Ben, but he never wanted to give the ball back.

When Ben came home from school, Buster went crazy.
The two of them played for ages and then Buster would sit next to Ben. When they went out, Buster would come too. He didn't like towns. He liked the woods near their house best, but he would go anywhere with Ben.

One day, Ben came home from school and rushed to see Buster. It was a hot day and Ben thought Buster was in the garden.
But Buster wasn't there.
Ben called him and
looked under every bush
in case he was hiding.

"Mum, Buster's not
here!" he shouted.

Mum came running out
and looked everywhere.
Ben was crying and

really scared – where could Buster be?

"Calm down Ben. We'll find him," said Mum.

They knocked on the doors of all the houses in the street to see if anyone had seen Buster, with no luck. One of the neighbours said that the window cleaner had been today and could have let Buster out by mistake. Ben was really worried.

"Could someone have stolen him, Mum?" he asked.

"No, I'm sure that hasn't happened. He's too scruffy for that."

Ben wasn't sure. Buster was the best dog in the world. Mum said she would tell the police that Buster was lost and put pictures of Buster everywhere saying he was missing. She would include a telephone number to contact them.

Hours went by and there was no sign of Buster. Ben couldn't go to sleep but Mum said he must try. As Ben lay in bed sobbing, he heard the doorbell ring. He heard voices and then a dog whined! He ran downstairs and there was Buster looking even scruffier than ever. Ben hugged him hard and looked up to see a man telling Mum where he had found him. It was the window cleaner telling Mum that Buster must have got out of the garden and climbed into his van, where he found some food. Buster had got stuck.

The window cleaner had gone home and into his garden.
He was cutting the grass and the hedge and hadn't heard Buster

barking. It was a good thing he had left the van windows open and that it was parked under a tree.

Much later the window cleaner heard a noise coming from the van and he found Buster.

He checked the name on his collar and drove him home.

Ben was so happy. The man smiled, pleased to see best friends together again.

Ben's mum said, "We need to make sure Buster can't go missing again. Now get to bed – it's really late."

Ben was finally able to get to sleep, but he kept a tight hold of Buster that night.

1. Why does the text say Buster *was <u>supposed to be</u> a cockapoo?*

Marks

Tick **one**.

He was a mix of a poodle and a cocker spaniel. ☐

He was funny. ☐

His coat was too curly and his ears weren't right. ☐

1

10 MINS

Marks

2. What funny things did Buster do? **Find** and **copy three** different facts about him.

1. _____

_____

2. _____

_____

3. _____

_____

1

3. What did Ben and his mum do together to look for Buster?

_____

_____

_____

1

4. What did a neighbour say could have happened to Buster?

_____

_____

_____

1

5. What did Ben think could have happened to Buster?

_____

1

6. Read the paragraph beginning *Hours went by...*

Find and **copy one** word that means the same as <u>crying really hard</u>.

_____

_____

Marks

1

7. Why was it a *good thing* that the window cleaner parked his van under a tree and left the windows open?

_____

_____

_____

2

8. Why did Ben keep *a tight hold of Buster that night?*

_____

_____

_____

2

Well done! END OF READING TEST 1!

Test 2
Reading

HOW TO MAKE A PAPER KITE

These instructions will show you how to make a paper kite.

You will need:

an A4 piece of stiff paper or card

a drinking straw (or a wooden skewer for extra strength)

ribbon – about 3cm wide and approximately 30cm long

strong string

tape

a pencil

scissors

ruler

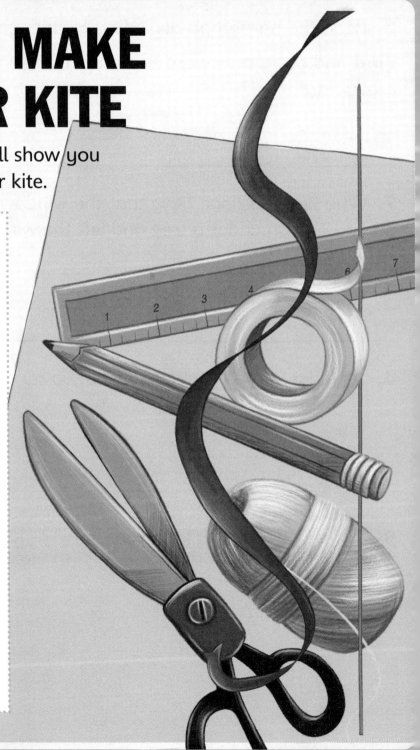

10 MINS

STEP 1 Fold the paper or card in half along the short side.

Fold

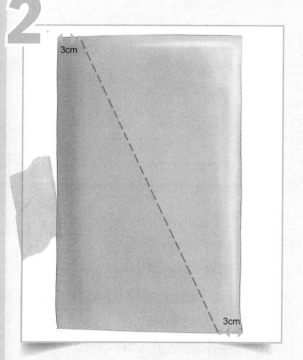
3cm

3cm

STEP 2 With the folded side on your left, make a mark at the top about 3cm along. Make another mark at the bottom 3cm in from the open side. Now draw a straight line with a pencil and ruler to connect these two marks.

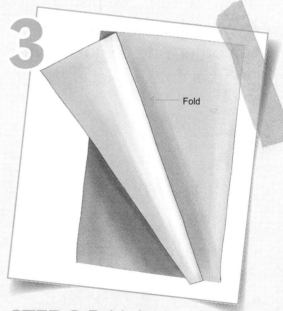
Fold

STEP 3 Fold the top half of the paper along the line you have just made.

10 MINS

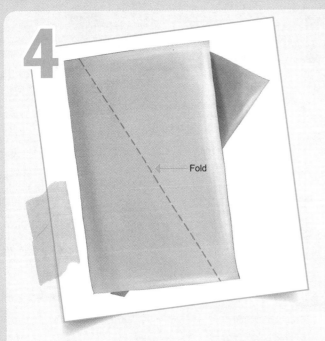

Fold

STEP 4 Turn the paper over and do the same on the other side so you have another folded piece.

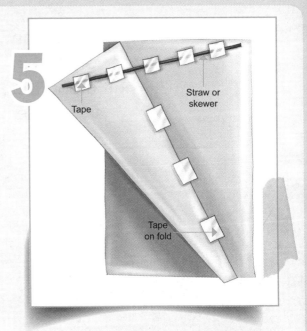

Tape

Straw or skewer

Tape on fold

STEP 5 Now tape along the fold to secure it on one side. Lay a straw or skewer along the kite as shown in the diagram and tape in place. You may need to cut the straw or skewer to fit. You may need to ask an adult to help.

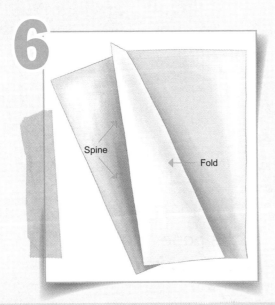

Spine

Fold

STEP 6 Turn the kite over and straighten the spine of the kite as shown. You will need to add a fold here so that the spine stands up vertically when the kite is face down.

7

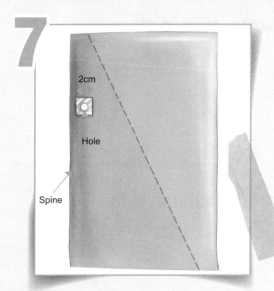

2cm

Hole

Spine

STEP 7 Mark a spot about one third of the way down the spine (as shown in the diagram) and about 2cm from the edge. Put tape over this mark. You need to make a hole where this mark is. Ask an adult to help. Tie your string through this hole and make a good knot.

8

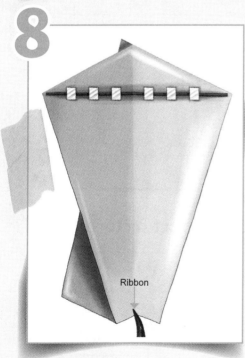

Ribbon

STEP 8 Tape a length of ribbon to the back of the kite at the bottom to make the tail. Now fly your kite! It is very light so best to do this on a day when it is not too windy.

Marks

1. Why might a wooden skewer be better than a straw for the kite?

_____

_____

_____

1

2. Look at step 2. What do you need a pencil and ruler for here?

_____

_____

_____

1

3. Look at step 6. Why do the instructions tell you to *straighten* the spine?

_____

_____

1

4. Draw lines to match each word to the correct picture.

| tape | hole | ribbon | skewer |

1

Marks

5. What is the ribbon for?

_____

_____

1

6. What will happen to the kite if it is too windy? Explain your answer.

_____

_____

_____

2

7. Why is it important to follow instructions, such as measuring with a ruler, carefully when making something like this? Explain your answer.

_____

_____

_____

_____

2

8. Why is the text written in numbered steps?

_____

_____

1

Well done! END OF READING TEST 2!

Test 3
Reading

Gran and the robber

Jack loved going to see his gran. He often went in the school holidays when his mum was at work. Gran always had interesting things for him to do and she told great stories.

One day in the summer holidays, Jack was at his gran's house when something very strange happened. Jack was busy making a game, sticking bits of cardboard together. His gran had a craft box full of things to cut out, stick and make.

Suddenly, Jack heard his gran shout out, "Oh no you don't!" He wondered who she was talking to. Before he could ask her, she shouted to him: "Stay where you are. I won't be long."

The front door banged and Jack went to look out the window. His gran, who usually walked slowly with a stick, was running down the drive into the road. A truck was backing out of the neighbour's house with all kinds of things piled in it. It looked like there was a television, a computer and other valuable things.

Gran rushed up and banged on the door of the truck. He heard her shout something. Then the truck stopped and the door opened. Jack was worried for his gran and wondered if he should go and help, but she had told him to stay where he was. Out of the truck jumped a nasty-looking man who was laughing at Gran. Oh dear, thought Jack, Gran won't like that.

The next thing Jack knew, Gran had grabbed hold of the man so that he couldn't move. The man looked scared now. All the noise had brought out another neighbour and soon Jack could hear a police car. The man couldn't get away – there were people everywhere. He was taken away by the policeman for stealing. Mrs Jones, who lived at the house, came back pleased to find her stolen things piled up by the front door, with nothing missing.

Gran walked slowly, as normal, up the drive and came in the front door.

"Gran, whatever happened?" said Jack.

"Well, a very naughty robber tried to steal Mrs Jones's things. I spotted him and knew she was out so I went to stop him."

"But Gran, weren't you frightened of him?" said Jack.

"No, I wasn't. I've never told you I used to be good at judo, have I? I don't like people like that. He didn't expect me to get him in a hold so he couldn't move."

"I didn't know you could run like that either, Gran."

"Well, I don't often. My knees are not as good as they used to be!"

"I think you're amazing. I'm going to call you Judo Gran from now on."

Gran just smiled and sat down with a cup of tea.

Marks

1. Find and **copy one** word in the story that means the same as <u>thief</u>.

_____

_____

1

2. Look at the paragraph beginning: *The front door banged...* Why is it surprising that Gran is running?

_____

_____

1

3. How do think the robber feels when he has been grabbed by Gran? Explain your answer.

_____

_____

_____

_____

_____

2

4. What causes the neighbour to come out?

_____

_____

1

5. Why is Mrs Jones pleased when she comes home?

_____

1

10 MINS

Marks

6. Write **two** things that Jack finds out about his gran that he didn't know before.

1. _____

2. _____

_____

1

7. Number the sentences below from 1–5 to show the order in which they happen in the story.

The robber is taken away by the policeman.	
Gran grabs hold of the man so he can't move.	
Jack is making a game.	
Gran rushes up and bangs on the door of the truck.	
The front door slams shut and Jack goes to look out the window.	

_____

1

8. What do you think Jack's mum might think or feel when she finds out what has happened? Explain your answer.

_____

_____

_____

_____

2

Well done! END OF READING TEST 3!

Test 4
Reading

Five ways to stay healthy

1. Keep active

To keep your body healthy and to grow strong, you need to spend at least one hour a day being active.

Try walking, or riding a scooter. You should also do some exercise that gets you out of breath, such as running, cycling, dancing or playing football.

2. Drink water

You need to drink about a litre of water a day to stay healthy. You should drink more if you are exercising, or if the weather is hot.

A lot of other drinks contain sugar, which can be bad for your teeth. Fizzy drinks are very bad for you as they have the most sugar. Even fruit juice has lots of sugar in it. A cup of apple juice can have six teaspoons of sugar in it. So pack a water bottle wherever you go and drink plenty of it!

3. Eat fruit and vegetables

Fruit and vegetables are full of lots of things that your body needs to grow well. They also taste good!

Try to eat two pieces of fruit and five lots of vegetables every day. You could have fruit with your breakfast and put vegetable sticks in your lunch box. Try adding fruit to your yoghurt, or put mushrooms, sweetcorn or peppers on top of your pizza.

4. Eat healthy snacks

Try not to eat snacks such as chips, crisps or cakes. These have too much salt or sugar in them. Snack on fruit and vegetables instead, which are much better for you. Or, if you are very hungry, have a hard-boiled egg, or a slice of wholemeal toast.

5. Switch off the screen

You should not spend more than two hours a day looking at a screen of any kind – including TV. When you do this, you are sitting still – not being active. This can lead to children becoming unfit.

10 MINS

Marks

1. **Find** and **copy three** kinds of exercise that are good for you.

1. _____

2. _____

3. _____

_____

1

2. What does fruit juice contain that is bad for your teeth?

_____

_____

1

3. What **two** things could you have for a snack, if you are very hungry?

1. _____

2. _____

_____

2

4. Look at tip 5: *Switch off the screen.*

What is the maximum time you should spend looking at a screen?

_____

1

5. Explain why you should not look at a screen too long.

Marks

_____

_____

_____

_____

1

6. Which of these statements are correct? Find the information in the text and tick **true** or **false**.

	True	False
You should do about one hour of exercise a day.		
You need to drink lots of fruit juice each day.		
You should eat one portion of fruit or vegetables a day.		
Some snack foods have too much salt or sugar in them.		

2

7. Describe **two** things that could happen to a child who drinks fizzy drinks, doesn't eat fruit or vegetables, doesn't exercise, and watches TV all the time. Explain your answer.

_____

_____

2

The Slug

Early one morning he started to slide
Across the garden freshly dug
Went the slimy slippery slug

In through a crack and into the house
Slowly moving along the rug
Went the slimy slippery slug

Behind the cupboard and onto the jug
Silently climbing up and up
Went the slimy slippery slug

Then right on top of the best blue mug
Slithering smoothly round and round
Went the slimy slippery slug

Back he went where he had come
Down the mug and past the jug
Went the slimy slippery slug

Leaving his trail all over the rug
Into the garden freshly dug
Went the slimy slippery slug

By Wendy Jolliffe

1. Look at the first verse. What time of day do you think it is when the slug begins to move?

_____

_____

Marks

1

2. Find and **copy three** words that appear together and begin with the same sound.

1. _____

2. _____

3. _____

_____

1

3. How does the slug get into the house?

_____

_____

1

4. Find and **copy one** word that describes how the slug climbs *up and up*.

_____

_____

1

5. How would anyone know that the slug has been in the house?

_____

1

10 MINS

	Marks

6. *Leaving his trail all over the rug*

Circle **one** word that means the same as *trail* in the poem:

[footpath] [route] [marks]

1

7. List **four** words you can find in the poem that rhyme with slug.

1. _____ 2. _____ 3. _____ 4. _____

1

8. Number the sentences 1–5 to show the order of the slug's journey.

He left a trail over the rug.	
He went behind the cupboard and onto the jug.	
He went back into the garden.	
He slid down the mug and past the jug.	
He came in through a crack.	

1

9. How do you think the person who lives in the house will feel when they see the slug trail? Explain your answer.

_____

_____

2

Well done! END OF READING TEST 5!

4 NEWS REPORT Tuesday. January 23, 2018

Scarborough's windy cliff tops

DANGEROUS RESCUE

A Year 3 school trip for children from Foss Bridge Primary School in York went badly wrong last Friday. <u>By **Rachel Smith**</u>

The children went on a school trip to Scarborough. They were learning about the coastline and the castle. Unfortunately, not long after they arrived, disaster struck. It was a very windy day and the children had been told to put on their coats, hats and gloves. They then walked along the cliff path down to the shore. The path is used by hundreds of people every day and no accidents have happened before. However, on Friday, a gust of wind took one of the children's hats and blew it over the cliff top. Quickly, the boy who had lost his hat – Sam – reached over the cliff to get it and he fell. To the horror of his teacher, he fell a terrible four metres down the cliff. Then he got stuck on a rock.

"Hold on tight! We will get help!" the teacher called to Sam. Then she took the rest of the children to safety and called the emergency services.

5 **NEWS REPORT** Tuesday. January 23, 2018

A helicopter was sent on its way to rescue Sam. Everyone was worried that Sam would fall further before the helicopter arrived. Just then, two young men walked past. They were going to climb the rocks further down and had ropes. They could see there was a problem and offered to help. One man secured a rope at the top of the cliff. The other man carefully abseiled down the cliff, using the rope. He quickly reached Sam and tied a rope round him. Then slowly the two men pulled Sam up the cliff to safety.

Just then, everyone heard the helicopter. The teacher telephoned the emergency services to explain that the boy was safe.

Emergency services responded to the call by helicopter

The children all waved at the helicopter and the pilot waved back. The two young men who had saved Sam said goodbye and went on to continue their climbing. The teacher didn't have time to thank them. The children were able to carry on with the trip and then Sam's mum came to make sure he was all right.

The school is offering a reward to the two brave young men who helped Sam. Anyone who knows them is asked to get in touch. The head teacher said, "We are so grateful for such bravery. This could have been a terrible accident, but thanks to these men everything was fine."

Marks

1. **Find** and **copy** the name of the place the Year 3 children were visiting on their school trip.

_____

_____

1

2. What were the children learning about?

Tick **two**.

the castle ☐   the town ☐

the weather ☐   the coastline ☐

1

3. How did the boy fall over the cliff?

_____

_____

1

4. Look at the paragraph beginning: *The children went on a school trip...*

Find and **copy four** words or phrases from the paragraph that tell you something bad happened.

1. _____

2. _____

3. _____

4. _____

2

Marks

5. Look at the paragraph beginning: *"Hold on tight!..."*

Write **two** things the teacher did to help Sam or the other children.

1. _____

2. _____

_____

1

6. Why was it a good thing that the two men were going past on their way to go rock climbing?

_____

_____

_____

1

7. Find and **copy one** word that means <u>climbed down a steep cliff using a rope</u>.

_____

_____

1

8. Why is the head teacher offering a reward in the newspaper?

_____

_____

_____

2

Well done! END OF READING TEST 6!

Fossil hunting

Alfie loved dinosaurs. He had collected books, models and pictures since he was four years old. He was now seven and he was interested in fossils because they could tell you about dinosaurs and other animals and plants from millions of years ago.

One day, Alfie's dad asked him if he would like to go on a fossil hunt at the seaside.

"Yes please!" said Alfie, very excitedly.

So, the next Saturday, Alfie put his fossil-hunting book in a bag and they set off with a bucket, a small hammer and a magnifying glass to help spot the fossils. Alfie's dad had checked to find out what time the tide was out as he said it was best to look then. They drove to the seaside, parked the car and walked down to the beach. They began by looking at the bottom of the cliff, near where the water comes in at high tide. As they walked along, Alfie's dad told Alfie to look for rocks that were a strange shape and had marks on them.

He told him that he may need to tap the rocks with a small hammer, but must be very careful not to damage the fossils.

Dad knew all about rocks.

It was not long before they found a strange-looking rock. Dad tapped it carefully. It split apart and revealed a fossil shaped like a spiral shell.

"This is an ammonite, Alfie," Dad explained. "This used to be a sea creature that lived at the same time as dinosaurs!"

"Wow," said Alfie, "that's great! Can we find some more?"

Over the next hour, Alfie and his dad found another ammonite. Then they sat down on the rocks to eat their lunch. Alfie was staring at the different rocks.

"Why has that rock got ripples, Dad?"

"They are fossilised ripples in the sand," said Dad.

"Wait a minute," said Dad. "Look at this!" He used the magnifying glass to look closely.

There in the rock was the shape of three dinosaur toes.
Alfie looked, too.

"Dad, where could they have come from?"

"I think they are marks from dinosaurs who walked here long ago."

"That's amazing!" said Alfie.

They took lots of photos and Alfie carefully traced over the fossil with a pencil and paper. Dad said this was called a rubbing.

"It's a pity we can't take the footprint home," said Alfie.

"Well, we have photos and a rubbing, don't we? I expect other people will find this and be excited like us."

When Alfie got home, he put his fossils in his bedroom. Dad told him he was a proper palaeontologist. When Alfie found out this meant a scientist who investigates fossils, he was very pleased. He decided he was going to be a palaeontologist when he grew up.

Marks

1. Where is a good place to look for fossils?

_____

_____

1

2. **Find** and **copy four** things Alfie and his dad take with them to help look for fossils.

1. _____

2. _____

3. _____

4. _____

_____

1

3. Alfie's dad says you have to be very careful when using a hammer on the rocks. Why is this?

_____

_____

1

4. How many ammonites do they find?

_____

_____

1

5. What do they find that showed that dinosaurs had walked in that place?

_____

1

Marks

6. Draw lines to match each word to the correct meaning.

Word	Meaning

ammonite

the remains, or signs, of a prehistoric plant or animal

palaeontologist

a spiral-shaped fossil that was a sea creature

fossil

a scientist who studies fossils

1

7. Dad says Alfie is a *proper palaeontologist*. Why does he say this?

_____

_____

_____

_____

2

8. Do you think Alfie will become a palaeontologist when he grows up? Explain your answer using evidence from the text.

_____

_____

_____

2

Well done! END OF READING TEST 7!

The Crocodile

How doth the little crocodile
    Improve his shining tail,
And pour the waters of the Nile
    On every golden scale!

How cheerfully he seems to grin,
    How neatly spread his claws,
And welcomes little fishes in,
    With gently smiling jaws!

By Lewis Carroll

1. Look at the first line of the poem. **Find** and **copy one** word that means <u>does</u>.

_____

_____

Marks

1

2. What part of the crocodile's body is *shining*?

_____

_____

1

3. Where does the crocodile live?

_____

_____

1

4. What colour are the crocodile's scales? Circle the correct answer.

red   golden   blue

_____

1

5. *How cheerfully he seems to grin!*

Why does the poet use the word *seems* here?

_____

_____

1

6. What does the crocodile eat?

_____

1

10 MINS

Marks

7. Are the crocodile's jaws really gentle? Give a reason for your answer.

_____

_____

_____

1

8. Draw lines to match each word to the correct meaning.

Word   **Meaning**

scales   bony plates that cover
                      the crocodile's body

cheerfully   smile

grin   happily

1

9. Is this a nice, friendly crocodile? Explain your answer, using evidence from the poem.

_____

_____

_____

_____

2

Well done! END OF READING TEST 8!

Polar bears

Polar bears are very large animals that live in the frozen Arctic where it can get as cold as minus 50 degrees Celsius. The scientific name for a polar bear is *ursus maritimus*, which means sea bear.

Male polar bears can weigh up to 700 kilograms and be over 3 metres tall on their hind legs. Females are half the size. Polar bears are the largest meat-eating animals on Earth. Their skin is actually black and their fur is transparent. Their fur reflects visible light which makes them appear white. This helps them to blend in with the snow. They have small ears and tails which stops them losing heat.

Baby polar bears are only about 30 centimetres long and weigh about 500 grams when they are born. This is about the same as a guinea pig. The cubs spend the first four or five months in a den. They stay with their mother for about two years in order to learn how to survive.

Polar bears eat seals and hunt for them on the ice. They wait next to breathing holes in the ice for seals to come out. Then they hit them and hook them with their claws. The bears have very good eyesight and an even better sense of smell – they can smell seals over a kilometre away! They also eat a kind of seaweed, called kelp, as well as fish and sea birds. At times of the year when there is not much food, polar bears can go into a kind of hibernation.

Polar bears have two coats to keep them warm, as well as a thick layer of blubber all over their body. The only parts of their body with no fur are their foot pads and the tip of the nose.

Polar bears can move quickly and reach speeds of 40 kilometres an hour on land and 10 kilometres an hour in water. They have strong legs and huge front paws, which they use as paddles for swimming. Their toes are good for walking on snow as they have claws which dig into the snow to help them grip.

There are over 20,000 polar bears in the world. However, scientists think there could be far fewer polar bears by 2050. This is because the world's climate is getting warmer and the ice in the Arctic is melting. This means there is less ice for the bears to hunt on.

Marks

1. What colour is the skin of a polar bear?

_____

_____

1

2. How do baby polar bears learn to survive?

_____

_____

1

3. What skills or senses does a polar bear have that help it to catch seals? Name **two** and explain how each helps the bear.

1. _____

2. _____

_____

2

4. Name **three** things that polar bears eat.

1. _____

2. _____

3. _____

_____

1

5. Why is blubber important to polar bears?

_____

_____

1

10 MINS

Marks

6. How fast can a polar bear swim?

_____

_____

1

7. Draw lines to match each word the correct meaning.

Word	**Meaning**
	thick layer of fat
transparent	
blubber	a deep sleep some animals have through the winter
hibernation	
	see-through

1

8. Explain why the future does not look very good for polar bears.

_____

_____

_____

_____

2

Well done! END OF READING TEST 9!

42

Violent volcanoes

A volcano is like a mountain with a big hole in the middle. The hole leads down to hot liquid rock inside the Earth.

When a volcano erupts, the hot liquid rock comes pouring out. When the liquid rock is inside the Earth, it is called magma. When the magma explodes out of the Earth, it is called lava. Lava can be very, very hot – up to 1000 degrees Celsius. It contains poisonous gases. Lots of ash often comes out of the volcano with the lava. When the lava stops flowing, it becomes hard and forms rocks.

There are over 1000 volcanoes in the world and many are under the sea. Volcanoes can be active, which means they are likely to erupt.

They can be dormant, which means they have not erupted for a long time. Or they can be extinct, which means they will not erupt any more.

Interesting facts about volcanoes

- A large volcanic eruption can destroy a whole forest.
- The largest volcano on land is Mauna Loa. This is on an island called Hawaii.
- The ash cloud from volcanoes can be dangerous. It can make it difficult for people to breathe. It is also difficult for planes to fly through the ash cloud.
- The tallest volcano we know of is on the planet Mars.
- There are no active volcanoes in the UK.
- The largest volcano in Europe is called Mount Etna.

Marks

1. Find and **copy one** word that means the same as <u>hot liquid rock inside Earth</u>.

_____

_____

 1

2. Lava and gases come out of a volcano. What also often comes out?

_____

 1

10 MINS

Marks

3. Explain why lava is so dangerous.

_____

_____

_____

_____

2

4. Label the diagram correctly with the following words:

    lava   magma   rocks formed from cooled lava

_____

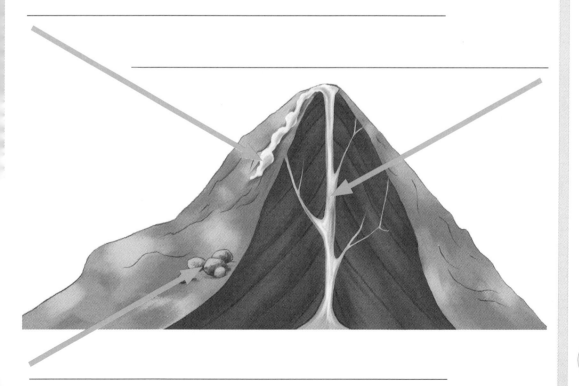

_____

2

5. What is the meaning of the word *dormant*?

_____

_____

1

6. Where is the largest land volcano in the world?

_____

_____

1

7. What is the largest volcano in Europe called?

_____

_____

1

8. Tick **true** or **false** for each statement about volcanoes.

Statement	True	False
Lava is very, very cold.		
There are no volcanoes in the sea.		
There is a very tall volcano on Mars.		
Planes find it difficult to fly through ash clouds.		

2

Well done! END OF READING TEST 10!

Answers
Reading

Q	Mark scheme for Reading Test 1: Ben and Buster	Marks
1	**Award 1 mark** for: His coat was too curly and his ears weren't right.	1
2	**Award 1 mark** for any three facts, such as: He would run around in circles chasing his tail, he would bark at trees when it was windy, he loved to play ball but never wanted to give the ball back.	1
3	**Award 1 mark** for: Ben and his mum went to all the houses in the street to ask if anyone had seen Buster.	1
4	**Award 1 mark** for: The neighbour said that the window cleaner had been today and could have let Buster out by mistake.	1
5	**Award 1 mark** for: Ben thought someone could have stolen Buster.	1
6	**Award 1 mark** for: sobbing	1
7	**Award 2 marks** for an answer that includes an explanation that it was a hot day and dogs can die in hot cars. **Award 1 mark** for an answer that includes one of these points. For example: It was a hot day.	2
8	**Award 2 marks** for an answer that explains that Ben was scared Buster might disappear again and that he is holding him tightly so this can't happen. **Award 1 mark** for an answer without a full explanation, such as: Ben is scared Buster might disappear again.	2
	TOTAL	10

Q	Mark scheme for Reading Test 2: How to make a paper kite	Marks
1	**Award 1 mark** for an answer such as: A wooden skewer would be stronger than a straw.	1
2	**Award 1 mark** for: to draw a line to connect the two marks	1
3	**Award 1 mark** for an answer that shows an understanding of the meaning of 'straight' and explains that if the kite is not straight, it will not fly properly. For example: If the spine of the kite isn't straight, the whole kite will be wonky and it won't fly properly.	1
4	**Award 1 mark** for all four words matched to the correct picture: tape hole ribbon skewer	1
5	**Award 1 mark** for: the tail of the kite	1
6	**Award 2 marks** for an answer that explains that the kite will probably break, and gives a detailed explanation using information from the text. For example: The kite will probably fall apart because it is very light and made of thin materials that aren't very strong. **Award 1 mark** for an answer with a simple explanation, such as: The kite will break because it is light.	2
7	**Award 2 marks** for an answer that explains that without careful measuring and folding the kite will be the wrong shape, or not secured properly, and so the kite might fall apart or will not work. **Award 1 mark** for an answer without an explanation. For example: The kite won't work.	2
8	**Award 1 mark** for an answer that shows an understanding that this is an instruction text. For example: It is telling you how to do something in the right order.	1
	TOTAL	10

Q	Mark scheme for Reading Test 3: Gran and the robber	Marks
1	**Award 1 mark** for: robber	1
2	**Award 1 mark** for: Gran normally walks slowly with a stick.	1
3	**Award 2 marks** for an answer that explains a feeling with an explanation. For example: The robber is surprised because he wouldn't have expected to be grabbed by an old lady. OR The robber is scared because he has been caught, and so might go to prison. **Award 1 mark** for a feeling without an explanation.	2
4	**Award 1 mark** for: all the noise (that Gran and the robber are making)	1
5	**Award 1 mark** for: Mrs Jones is pleased because the robber hasn't been able to steal any of her things.	1
6	**Award 1 mark** for both of the following: 1. She can run. 2. She used to be good at judo.	1

7

Award 1 mark for all boxes numbered correctly.

The robber is taken away by the policeman.	5
Gran grabs hold of the man so he can't move.	4
Jack is making a game.	1
Gran rushes up and bangs on the door of the truck.	3
The front door slams shut and Jack goes to look out the window.	2

Marks: 1

8

Award 2 marks for an answer that predicts what Mum might think or feel with an explanation based on the text. For example:
- Jack's mum might be surprised because she would not be expecting there to be a robbery.

OR
- Jack's mum might be impressed that Gran has caught a robber because it was very brave for her to have fought a robber.

Award 1 mark for a prediction without an explanation.

Marks: 2

	TOTAL	10

Q	Mark scheme for Reading Test 4: Five ways to stay healthy	Marks
1	**Award 1 mark** for any three of the following: • walking • riding a scooter • running • cycling • dancing • playing football • exercise that gets you out of breath	1
2	**Award 1 mark** for: sugar	1
3	**Award 1 mark** for both: hard-boiled egg, slice of wholemeal toast	1
4	**Award 1 mark** for: two hours a day	1
5	**Award 2 marks** for an answer such as: Looking at a screen for more than two hours a day means you are not active and this can lead to being unfit. **Award 1 mark** for an answer that refers only to not being active or being unfit.	2
6	**Award 2 marks** for four correct answers. **Award 1 mark** for two or three correct answers. 		True	False
You should do about one hour of exercise a day.	✓	
You need to drink lots of fruit juice each day.		✓
You should eat one portion of fruit or vegetables a day.		✓
Some snack foods have too much salt or sugar in them.	✓			2
7	**Award 2 marks** for an answer that gives two consequences and an explanation. For example: They could have bad teeth from drinking too many sugary drinks and if they don't eat enough fruit and vegetables, their bodies might not grow well. **Award 1 mark** for an answer that gives one consequence and an explanation, or two consequences but no explanation. For example: If they don't do enough exercise, they will be unfit. OR They won't grow properly and they could be unfit.	2
	TOTAL	10

49

Q	Mark scheme for Reading Test 5: The Slug	Marks
1	**Award 1 mark** for: early in the morning	1
2	**Award 1 mark** for: slimy, slippery, slug	1
3	**Award 1 mark**: through a crack	1
4	**Award 1 mark** for: silently	1
5	**Award 1 mark** for an answer that refers to trails. For example: They will know because there are slug trails everywhere.	1
6	**Award 1 mark** for: marks	1
7	**Award 1 mark** for: dug, rug, jug, mug	1
8	**Award 1 mark** for all sentences in the correct order: | He left a trail over the rug.	4
He went behind the cupboard and onto the jug.	2
He went back into the garden.	5
He slid down the mug and past the jug.	3
He came in through a crack.	1		1
9	**Award 2 marks** for an answer that gives a reaction and a reason for this, based on the poem. For example: They will be annoyed because the slug has left a messy trail over so many different things in the house. **Award 1 mark** for a reaction without a reason, such as: They will be annoyed.	2
	TOTAL	10

Q	Mark scheme for Reading Test 6: Dangerous rescue	Marks
1	**Award 1 mark** for: Scarborough	1
2	**Award 1 mark** for both ticked: the coastline, the castle	1
3	**Award 1 mark** for an answer such as: He was trying to get his hat which had blown off.	1
4	**Award 2 marks** for any four of the following: • disaster (struck) • unfortunately • he fell • to the horror of his teacher/horror • terrible/terrible four metres • he got stuck on a rock **Award 1 mark** for any two or three of the words/phrases listed above.	2
5	**Award 1 mark** for any two of the following: • She checked Sam was OK. • She rang the emergency services. • She got the rest of the class to safety.	1
6	**Award 1 mark** for an answer such as: They saw that there was a problem and could help.	1
7	**Award 1 mark** for: abseiling	1
8	**Award 2 marks** for an answer that includes an explanation. For example: The head teacher and the school want to thank the young men and they need to ask the newspaper to help because they don't know the men's names or who they are. **Award 1 mark** for an answer without an explanation. For example: They want to thank the men.	2
	TOTAL	10

Q	Mark scheme for Reading Test 7: Fossil hunting	Marks
1	**Award 1 mark** for any of the following answers: at the beach, near the cliffs, at the high tide mark, at the seaside	1
2	**Award 1 mark** for all four correct: a bucket, a hammer, a magnifying glass, a fossil-hunting book	1
3	**Award 1 mark** for: Because you could damage the fossil with the hammer.	1
4	**Award 1 mark** for: two	1
5	**Award 1 mark** for: They find prints of dinosaur toes in the rock.	1
6	**Award 1 mark** for all three matched correctly: ammonite ⟶ a spiral-shaped fossil that was a sea creature palaeontologist ⟶ a scientist who studies fossils fossil ⟶ the remains, or signs, of a prehistoric plant or animal	1
7	**Award 2 marks** for an answer such as: Alfie has shown that he is very interested in fossils. Dad thinks Alfie has done a good job looking for and studying fossils, which is what a palaeontologist does. **Award 1 mark** for: Because Alfie has been looking for fossils and studying them, like a palaeontologist. Do not award any marks for: Because Alfie has been acting like a palaeontologist.	2
8	**Award 2 marks** for an answer that includes two reasons from the text to support an opinion. For example: I think Alfie will become a palaeontologist because he has collected things about dinosaurs for years and he was excited about finding the fossils. **Award 1 mark** for one reason.	2
	TOTAL	10

Q	Mark scheme for Reading Test 8: The Crocodile	Marks
1	**Award 1 mark** for: doth	1
2	**Award 1 mark** for: tail	1
3	**Award 1 mark** for: the (River) Nile	1
4	**Award 1 mark** for: golden	1
5	**Award 1 mark** for: To show he's not really grinning/smiling. (It's just the shape of his mouth.)	1
6	**Award 1 mark** for: fish	1
7	**Award 1 mark** for an answer such as: No – the jaws are dangerous, with big teeth to eat fish.	1
8	**Award 1 mark** for all three correct: scales ⟶ bony plates that cover the crocodile's body cheerfully ⟶ happily grin ⟶ smile	1
9	**Award 2 marks** for an answer that explains that the crocodile seems nice but is actually dangerous, with evidence to support. For example: The crocodile seems nice, because he is welcoming and grinning. But he isn't really nice and friendly because he has big claws and teeth, and eats the fish at the end. **Award 1 mark** for one point with evidence. For example: The crocodile isn't nice and friendly because it has big teeth and claws to eat things like fish.	2
	TOTAL	10

Q	Mark scheme for Reading Test 9: Polar bears	Marks
1	**Award 1 mark** for: black	1
2	**Award 1 mark** for an answer such as: They stay with their mother for two years (until they have learned how to survive).	1
3	**Award 2 marks** for an answer that refers to two characteristics and explains how each one helps the bear to catch seals: For example: • They have claws to hook the seals. • They have a good sense of smell and so know where seals are from over a kilometre away. **Award 1 mark** for referring to one characteristic with an explanation, or for naming two characteristics but with no explanation.	2
4	**Award 1 mark** for any three of: seals, kelp (sea weed), sea birds, fish	1
5	**Award 1 mark** for an answer such as: Blubber keeps them warm.	1
6	**Award 1 mark** for: 10 kilometres an hour	1
7	**Award 1 mark** for all three words matched to the correct meaning: transparent ——————▶ see-through blubber ——————▶ thick layer of fat hibernation ——————▶ a deep sleep some animals have through the winter	1
8	**Award 2 marks** for an answer that includes an explanation that the ice in the Arctic is melting and polar bears need to hunt on the ice. **Award 1 mark** for an answer that includes one of these points. For example: the ice in the Arctic is melting.	2
	TOTAL	10

Q	Mark scheme for Reading Test 10: Violent volcanoes	Marks
1	**Award 1 mark** for: magma	1
2	**Award 1 mark** for: ash (cloud)	1
3	**Award 2 marks** for an answer that includes both of the following reasons: The lava is very hot so would destroy plants and animals, and it also contains poisonous gases. **Award 1 mark** for an answer that refers to either the heat or the gases.	2
4	**Award 1 mark** for all three labels added correctly. <Design: add labelled diagram here when ready.>	1
5	**Award 1 mark** for: not erupted for a long time (dormant literally means 'sleeping')	1
6	**Award 1 mark** for: Hawaii	1
7	**Award 1 mark** for: Mount Etna	1
8	**Award 2 marks** for all four answers correct.<table><tr><th>Statement</th><th>True</th><th>False</th></tr><tr><td>Lava is very, very cold.</td><td></td><td>✓</td></tr><tr><td>There are no volcanoes in the sea.</td><td></td><td>✓</td></tr><tr><td>There is a very tall volcano on Mars.</td><td>✓</td><td></td></tr><tr><td>Planes find it difficult to fly through ash clouds.</td><td>✓</td><td></td></tr></table>**Award 1 mark** for two or three correct answers.	2
	TOTAL	10

Skills check

Reading

Words in context

Can you...

- read the word in a sentence to work out its meaning?
- think of words with similar meanings?
- write a sentence that contains a word, for example using the word 'stolen'.

What you need to know

- There may be more than one meaning for a word. You have to find the word, or phrase, that is nearest to the meaning of the word in a sentence.
- Sometimes you have to look for clues about the word's meaning by reading the whole sentence or paragraph.
- To answer questions about words you may be asked to match, underline, circle, tick, or write a few words of your own.

Example

> When Jack saw Gran grab the robber, and then put him in a hold, he was surprised. Gran normally had difficulties walking without a stick.

1. Circle **one** word that means the same as <u>hold</u>.

    grip   hug   lift

2. **Find** and **copy** the words that explain why Jack was surprised.

<u>Gran normally had difficulties walking without a stick.</u>

Skills check

Identifying key features

Can you...

- find the setting, characters and main events of a story?
- use titles and headings to find information quickly?
- use pictures, labels and captions to help you answer questions?
- think about how pieces of information are related to each other?

Retrieval of information

Can you...

- find information?
- copy accurately?

What you need to know

- 'Retrieval' means to find and write down.
- All the answers will be in the text. You just have to find them.
- The questions are in the order that the answers appear in the text.
- You may be asked to underline, circle, tick or find and copy information.

Example

It was teatime when Sam noticed that Barney was missing. He looked in her basket, on the sofa and on the rug but he wasn't there! He was about to shout to mum, when he heard a bark and he was surprised to find Barney on his bed.

1. What time of day was it when Sam thought Barney was missing?

Teatime (not a specific time)

2. Where did Barney usually sleep?

Her basket, the sofa or on the rug

3. Where was Barney when Sam found him? Why do you think he was surprised?

On his bed. He was surprised because he was not supposed to be there (or he was not usually there).

Skills check

Summarising main ideas

Can you...

- find the main ideas?
- state the main ideas?

What you need to know

- Main ideas are the most important parts of the text: pieces of information or a message (for example, from a poem) that the author wants you to know.
- To 'summarise' a text means to say what it is about in a few words.
- Summarising questions will ask you to find information from reading the whole text.
- Summary answers are usually short.
- You may be asked to circle, tick, underline or write a few words.

Example

Hedgehogs

Hedgehogs get their names because they look through hedges for worms and insects and make a noise like a pig. The name for a baby hedgehog is a hoglet. Hedgehogs have bad eyesight, but good hearing and smell. They have about 5000 spines and there are 17 different types of hedgehog. Hedgehogs in England hibernate, or go to sleep in the winter. They are good for the garden because they eat slugs and beetles that harm plants.

1. Summarise in a few words what this is about.

Information about hedgehogs.

'Hedgehogs' isn't enough to give the main idea.

Inference

Can you...

- use what you have already read to work out what might happen next?
- use clues in the text to work out what a character is like?
- link what you have read to other stories and experiences?

What you need to know

- Inferences are ideas or understanding that you have to work out. The author doesn't tell you.
- Inference questions could be about a character, place or a reason why something happens.
- 'Giving reasons' or 'using evidence from the text' means finding something from the text that explains your thoughts.
- Inference questions might be about the whole text or small parts of it.
- You may be asked to circle, tick, underline or write a few words.

Example

James liked looking for treasure. He was always digging in the garden or at the beach. His uncle had a metal detector which you hold over the ground and listen for a noise when it finds some metal. His uncle once found a very old coin that was worth a lot of money. James once went with his uncle hunting for treasure and asked if he could hold the detector. His uncle said it was difficult, but he could hold it with him and listen for the noise it made.

1. Why are metal detectors good for looking for treasure?

   Answers that explain that metal detectors help you find things buried in the ground.

2. Why did James's uncle say he could not hold the metal detector on his own?

It was difficult because it was heavy. It was also worth a lot of money.

   (not just because it was difficult)

Prediction

Can you...

- say what might happen?
- explain your reasons with evidence from the text?

What you need to know

- 'Predicting' means saying what you think will happen next.
- In order to predict, you need to find out what has already happened.
- Your prediction must be likely.
- Prediction questions can often require longer answers and are often worth more than one mark.

Example

> Stamford Bridge football team have done well this year. They have won all their games except one. They are playing York Wanderers this week who are behind them in points.

1. Based on this, who do you think will win the match this week?
   Give a reason for your answer using evidence from the text.

Stamford Bridge will win as they have won all but one game this year and York Wanderers are behind them in points.

Skills check

How information is related

Can you...

- show *where* information is related?
- explain *how* the information is related?

What you need to know

- These questions will ask you to find information from more than one paragraph.
- 'How information is related' means how the text is linked together.
- These questions may ask you to order events, show how themes run through a text or explain how beginnings link to endings.

Example

The bus stopped suddenly. The passengers on the bus had to hold on to something so they didn't fall and several people found their shopping went all over the bus. Everyone looked to see why it had stopped. It was not a bus stop. There in front of the bus was a large cow that had crossed the road without looking!

1. Read the first and last sentences. How do they link together?

The first sentence explains that the bus stopped suddenly. The final sentence explains what has caused it to stop.

Skills check

How meaning is enhanced

Can you...

- find *where* meaning is enhanced?
- explain *how* meaning is enhanced?

What you need to know

- 'Enhanced' means made better or made clearer.
- The main way to enhance meaning is to use types of language such as repeating the same sound, for example 'the slippery slimy slug'.
- You need to be able to say what the writer is trying to do and how he or she does it.
- You might be asked how a writer makes the reader feel, excitement, fear or sadness when reading a story.
- You will usually be asked to find evidence from the text and write about it.

Example

Alex woke up suddenly in the middle of the night. What was that strange noise? It sounded like a door opening slowly. He held his breath, opened one eye and peered into the darkness...

1. Why was Alex frightened?

He was woken up in the middle of the night by a strange noise.

2. **Find** and **copy** words from the story that show Alex wanted to stay very quiet.

He held his breath, opened one eye and peered into the darkness.

Skills check

Question types: selected

Selected questions don't ask you to write your own answer. For these questions you need to circle, tick or draw lines.

What you need to know

- Multiple-choice questions will ask you to tick a box (possibly in a table) or circle a word or phrase.
- Ranking or ordering questions will ask you to write numbers in boxes to order sentences.
- Matching questions will ask you to draw lines to make connections.
- Labelling questions will ask you to label the features or parts of a text.
- Read the instruction text carefully to ensure that you tick or circle the correct number of options: for example, does the instruction say *Tick one* or *Tick two*? If you tick too many or too few options, you may not get the mark.
- Read all the possible answers, find the relevant information in the text, and check each possibility before deciding on a final answer.
- Carefully cross out any answers you have ticked, circled or labelled in error.

Skills check

These questions require you to write a small amount of text. It might just be a word, phrase or a sentence.

What you need to know

- Find-and-copy questions require you to read the text and find a word, phrase or sentences from it that answers the question. You should copy the words exactly. Make sure you read the question carefully so you know which word(s) you are looking for.
- Short-response questions require a short answer (a word, phrase or sentence), which will often be in the text.
- These questions are testing your understanding of the text, not your general knowledge. The answer you give should always be based on what you have read in the test paper.
- Practise looking for key words in questions and finding these in the text.

There will be some questions that require a longer response and are awarded two marks. You may have to explain your answer. There will only be one or two questions like this in the test papers.

What you need to know

- Read the question carefully. It is important that you know when you need evidence from the text to support your answer.
- Practise reading questions that require longer answers and planning your answer.
- Try all these longer questions on the test paper, even if they seem difficult, as they are worth two marks. You could get one mark for an answer that is partly right.

Progress chart

Fill in your score in the table below to see how well you've done.

	Score
Test 1	
Test 2	
Test 3	
Test 4	
Test 5	
Test 6	
Test 7	
Test 8	
Test 9	
Test 10	
TOTAL	

Mark	
0–34	Good try! You need more practice in some topics – ask an adult to help you.
35–69	You're doing really well. Ask for extra help for any topics you found tricky.
70–100	You're a 10-Minute SATs Test reading star – good work!

GREAT WORK!

Reward Certificate

Well done!

You have completed all of the 10-Minute SATs Tests

Name: _____ Date: _____

SCHOLASTIC

Prepare for SATs Success

BOOSTER
Tests & Workbooks

Give SATs results an extra boost

978-1407-16853-1

978-1407-16858-6

978-1407-16848-7

978-1407-16085-6

978-1407-16843-2

978-1407-16081-8

CHALLENGE
Workbooks & Skills Tests

For children looking for extra stretch

978-1407-17649-9

978-1407-17543-0

978-1407-17553-9

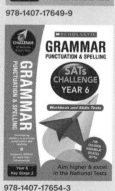

978-1407-17654-3

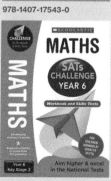

978-1407-17548-5

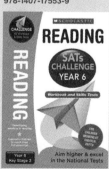

978-1407-17558-4

Find out more at www.scholastic.co.uk/assessment

QUICK TESTS FOR SATs SUCCESS

BOOST YOUR CHILD'S CONFIDENCE WITH 10-MINUTE SATs TESTS

- Bite-size mini SATs tests which take just 10 minutes to complete
- Covers key National Test topics
- Full answers and progress chart provided to track improvement
- Available for Years 1 to 6

Find out more at www.scholastic.co.uk